KeyEducation®

Social Skills
School Routines

Mini-Books to Teach Essential Social Skills

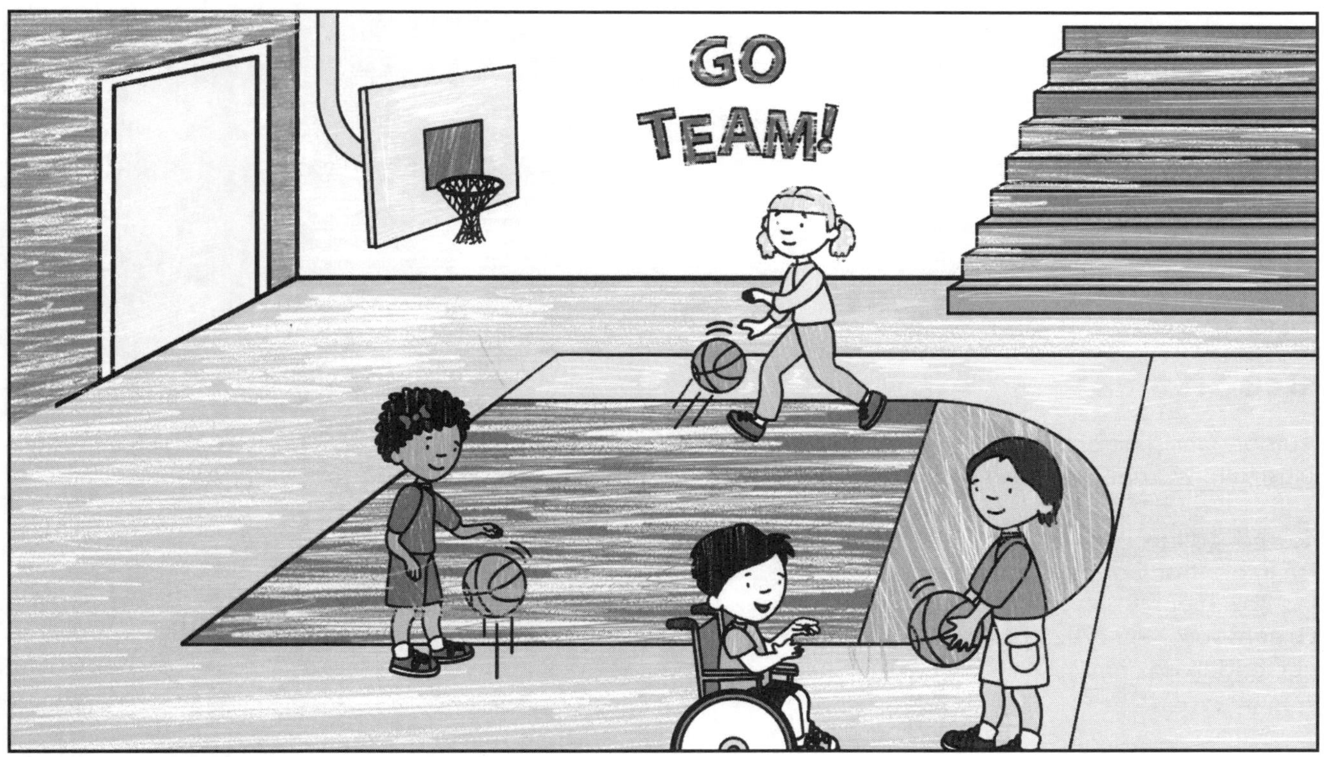

Carson Dellosa Education
Greensboro, North Carolina

Credits

Author: Christine Schwab
Illustrations: Pam Thayer, Julie Kinlaw, Erik Huffine, J.J. Rudisill

Key Education®
An imprint of Carson Dellosa Education
PO Box 35665
Greensboro, NC 27425 USA
carsondellosa.com

ISBN 978-1-4838-5697-1
01-335197784

Introduction

Social skills are important. They are like good manners. Using them properly makes it easier to relate to other people with positive outcomes. Children with age-appropriate social skills can more effectively communicate, make decisions, solve problems, create and maintain successful relationships, and manage their own behavior. A lack of age-appropriate social skills interferes with children's relationships with other children, their teachers, and their family members.

Social skills do not come naturally to all children. But, social skills can be shaped. Social narratives—short stories that focus on specific social skills or desired behaviors—are useful tools to this end. They can be written or modified to meet any specific challenge.

Ideas for Using
the Materials in This Book

Making the Mini-Books

This book focuses on tasks that are important in building essential skills. These pages present 13 mini-books that highlight and reinforce common behavior expectations. The illustrations are simple and printed in black and white so that children can color them. This interactive component helps children make the mini-books "their own" books.

The story pages are perforated and can be reproduced (two-sided) or assembled as single copies. Some children can cut apart and assemble the pages themselves, then staple the pages together on the left side of the books. (Check that the pages are in the correct order and help children if needed.) You may also choose to bind the books by using a hole punch and yarn or small metal rings.

Once the books are assembled, have children read their completed social narratives aloud. If a child cannot read independently, read the lines to the child. Following the first reading, have children "sign" their title pages and color the illustrations with crayons or markers. Reread the stories as needed. Over time, the narratives will become more familiar.

Repetition

New behaviors become more deeply ingrained each time they are practiced, so it is important to encourage children to read and reread their social narratives (aloud to another person). A goal chart is printed on the back page of each story to help children keep track of their progress toward a goal of reading the social story 10 times. The book concludes with award certificates for achievement and effort.

In This Book

Each mini-book in this book focuses on an important developmental social skill. They can be used in any order and as frequently as needed.

These social narratives are written in simple language so that they can be easily understood and assimilated. We hope they will prove to be an invaluable tool in shaping children's behavior.

Following the Rules

by ___________________________

Some rules tell me what I should do.
One rule is that I should sit in my seat for classwork.

(3)

(2) Every classroom has rules.
Rules help me know how to behave.

I should raise my hand to talk.
I should line up quietly for recess.
I should whisper in the library.

Some rules tell me what I should not do.
I should not touch stuff that is not mine.

5

It is important for me to follow the rules.
When I follow the rules, my teacher feels happy with me.

7

I should not run in the hallway.
I should not yell or make a lot of noise.
I should not hit people.

6

I will work on meeting
my goal - 10 ✔'s!

Make a ✔ each time you read your story.

On the Bus

by _______________________________

The bus has many seats.
I will sit down as soon as I get on the bus.
I cannot stand up when the bus is moving.

(3)

(2) Some days I ride the bus to school.
I like riding on my bus.

(4) It is important to pay attention to the bus driver.
I will follow the bus driver's rules.

I can talk to the other children on my bus.
Some of them are my friends.
I will talk quietly and stay in my seat.

5

Following the rules on the bus will keep me safe.
My family and I feel good when I am safe.

7

I will not yell or scream on the bus.
It is not safe when there is too much noise on the bus.

I will work on meeting
my goal - 10 ✔'s!

Make a ✔ each time you read your story.

Weather Delays

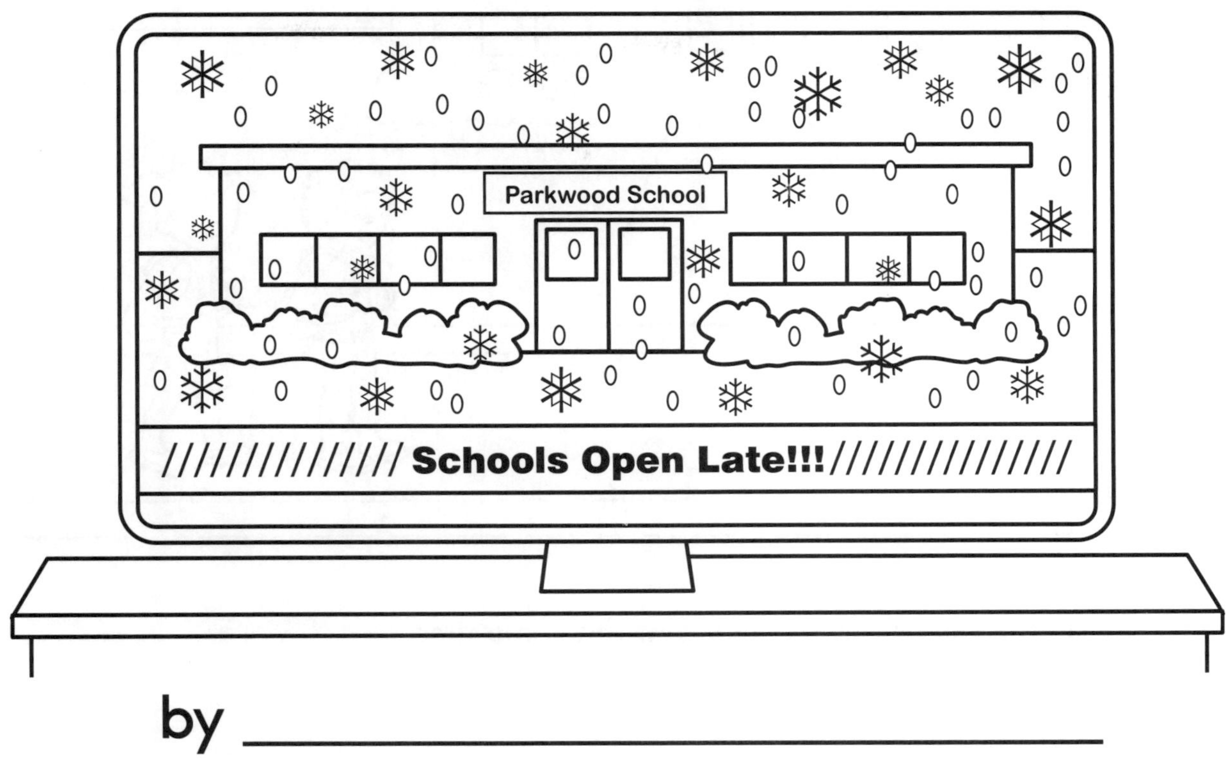

by _______________________

But, not everything stays the same all the time.
Sometimes my school might open late because of bad weather.

③

____

____

2 My school almost always starts at the same time.
I like when things stay the same.

When there is bad weather, my family will get a
phone call or hear about it on TV, the internet, or the radio.
4 There will be a new plan for the day.

When my school opens late, I will do my best to stay calm.
I know that nothing can be done about bad weather.

(5)

My family and my teachers are proud of me when I accept
changes calmly.

(7)

A late start means my class schedule will be different.
My teacher will give me a new schedule.
I will follow my new schedule calmly.

(6)

I will work on meeting
my goal - 10 ✔'s!

Make a ✔ each time you read your story.

Spring Break

		March		1 Friday	2 Saturday	
Sunday	Monday	Tuesday	Wednesday	Thursday	1 Friday	2 Saturday
3	4	5	6	7	8	9
10 Daylight Savings Time begins	11	12	13	14	15	16
17	18	19	20 Spring begins	21	22	23
24 / 31	25	26 **SPRING BREAK**	27	28	29	30

by _______________________________

When I am on spring break, I will not go to school.
I will stay at home.
My routines will change, but this is OK.

(3)

2

My school closes for spring break in March or April.
Spring break is when teachers and kids get a break from school.

I do not have to worry about my spring break schedule.
My family will help me understand the changes in my routine.

4

When it is spring break, I will get to play more.
I can read more books.
Maybe I can have my friends over to play with me.

(5)

Spring break is fun even if it changes my routines.
I will relax and do my best to have a good time.

(7)

6 If the weather is nice, I can play outside.
I might even go on an outing with my family.
For my spring break, I would like to go to _________________________.

I will work on meeting
my goal - 10 ✔'s!

Make a ✔ each time you read your story.

Announcements

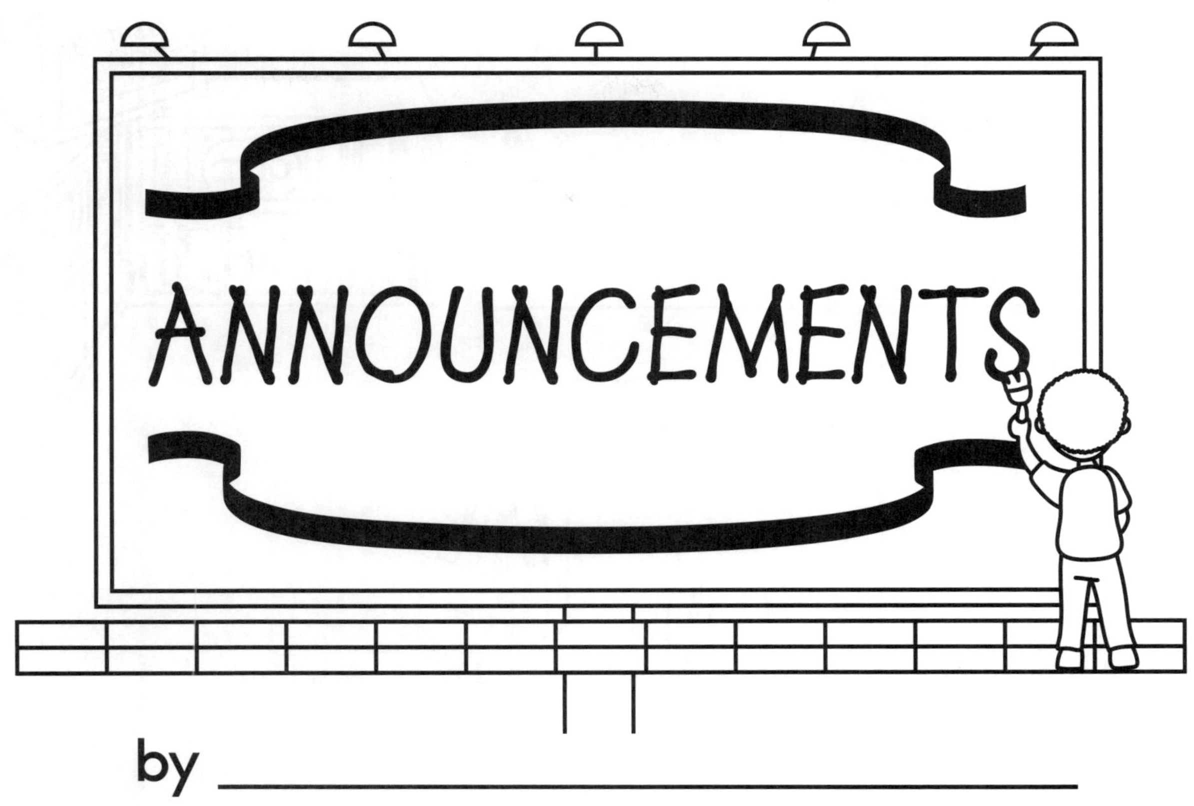

by ________________________________

Sometimes my teacher will give the announcements.
Sometimes they are given over the intercom or TV in my classroom.

(3)

(2) Announcements are made almost every day at my school.
The announcements tell me the school news.

(4) I should always pay close attention to the announcements.
The announcements are about important things.

Some announcements will tell me if school is starting late or closing early.
Maybe there will be a special assembly.

(5)

❀	❀	❀	May	❀	❀	❀
Sunday	Monday	Tuesday	Wednesday	Thursday	1 Friday	2 Saturday
3	4 Bookmobile	5	6 Chorus Try-outs	7	8 Early Dismissal	9
10	11 Art Show	12	13 Digital Day	14	15	16
17	18	19	20	21	22 Field Trip	23
24 / 31	25 Report Cards	26	27 Dance Recital	28	29	30

I can learn many important things by paying attention to the announcements.
I am happier when I know what is going to happen in my day.

(7)

(6) One announcement might tell me about a special outside event. Or, I might learn about a field trip.

I will work on meeting
my goal - 10 ✔'s!

Make a ✔ each time you read your story.

Substitute Teachers

by ___________________________

When my teacher cannot come to school, a substitute teacher will come to my class.
I will use good manners with my new teacher.

(3)

Sometimes my teacher cannot come to school.
My teacher might be sick.
Or, she might have something important to do.

2

It is important to remember the rules when a substitute teacher is in my classroom.
They are the same rules I follow with my regular teacher.

4

My substitute will be another nice teacher.
He can help me with my work.
He can answer my questions.

5

It is OK when a substitute is in my classroom.
My other teacher will be back soon.
My teacher feels happy when I behave for the substitute teacher.

7

If I have a problem or if I feel sick, I can talk to the substitute teacher.
He will help me.

I will work on meeting
my goal - 10 ✔'s!

Make a ✔ each time you read your story.

Assemblies

by _______________________

When it is time to go to the assembly, my teacher will tell us to line up.
I will get in line quickly and quietly.

(3)

(2) Sometimes my class goes to a special assembly.
Assemblies are usually held in a large room like the gym.

Usually, the whole school comes to the assembly.
We all sit with our teachers.
I will stay with my class and my teacher.

Before the assembly, the principal might make important announcements.
I will sit quietly and pay attention.

(5)

Going to an assembly is fun.
I feel happy when I can go to special assemblies with my friends at school.

(7)

During the assembly, people might sing or dance or tell stories.
I will sit quietly and pay attention.
When other people clap, I will clap too.

6

I will work on meeting
my goal - 10 ✔'s!

Make a ✔ each time you read your story.

Special Classes

by ___________________________

One of my special classes is PE.
I also go to music and art classes.
There are special teachers in each of these classes.

③

 **2** Most of the time I stay in the same classroom with my teacher.
But, sometimes I have special classes in other classrooms.

Sometimes I work with other teachers.
I might work with someone who helps me with my reading.
Another teacher can help me practice my speech.

4

When I am in my special classes, I will follow the rules.
Even if they are not my usual rules, I will follow them.

(5)

When I listen to my teachers and follow their rules, they feel happy
with me.
I feel happy too!

(7)

6 I will always listen to my teachers when they are talking.
I will sit quietly and keep my hands to myself in all of my classrooms.

I will work on meeting
my goal - 10 ✔'s!

Make a ✔ each time you read your story.

Going to the Library

by _______________________________

The library is a quiet place.
It is important that nobody makes loud noises in the library.
This helps people to study and read.

3

I like to go to the library.
There are lots of books there.
A book I like to read is ________________________________ .

 2

In the library, I will get books quietly.
I will pick one or two books that interest me.
Or, I will look for books that my teacher wants me to read.

4

I will find a place to sit down and read my books.
I will stay in my seat and read quietly.

(5)

When I am quiet in the library, everyone can enjoy reading books.
My teacher and the librarian feel happy when I am quiet in
the library.

(7)

(6) If I have something to say to my teacher
or my friends, I will whisper.
When I whisper, I will not interrupt other readers.

I will work on meeting
my goal - 10 ✔'s!

Make a ✔ each time you read your story.

Field Trips

by _______________________________

When we go on field trips, we will ride the bus.
I must remember to stay in my seat.
I will always sit down while the bus is moving.

(3)

2

Sometimes my class goes on field trips.
We visit interesting places on field trips.

It is OK to talk to my friends on the bus.
I will talk to them in a quiet voice.
I will not yell or scream.

4

When the bus stops for our field trip, I will get in line.
I will wait for my teacher to tell me what to do next.

⑤

Field trips are fun.
When I follow the rules, I will see new places and learn new things.

⑦

(6) There are usually parent helpers on field trips.
I will follow their rules too.
If my teacher is busy, one of them can help me.

I will work on meeting
my goal - 10 ✔'s!

Make a ✔ each time you read your story.

Grades

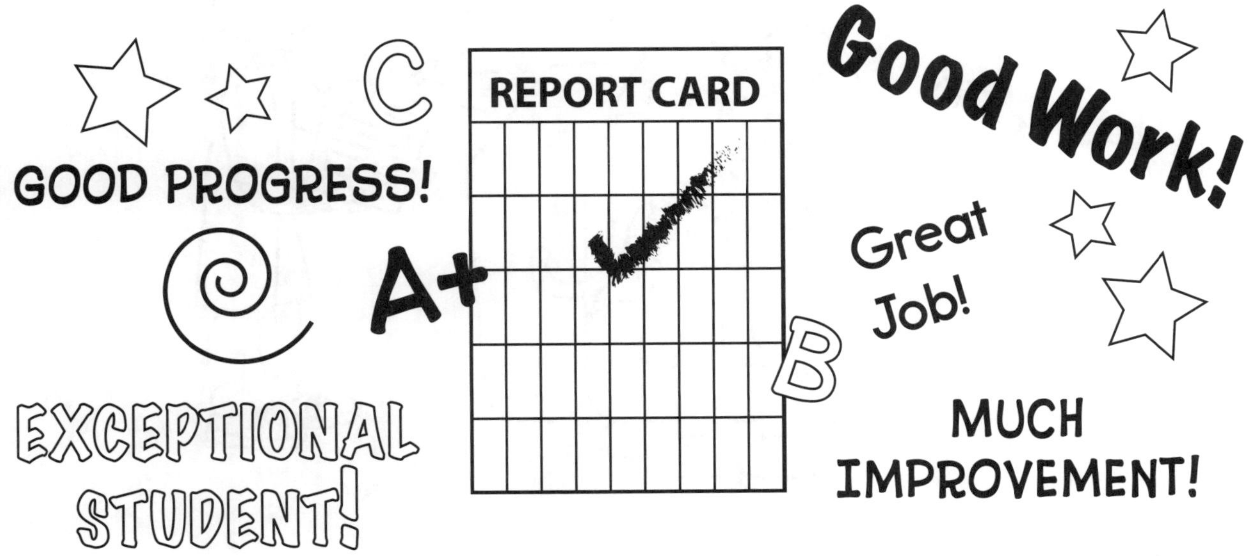

by _______________________

Grades tell me if I did a good job on my schoolwork.
Grades tell me how well I learned something new.

(3)

2 Sometimes I get stars or good-work stickers on my schoolwork.
Sometimes my teacher writes a grade on it.

A good grade might be an A, B, or C.
If I get a D or an F, it means that I have more to learn.

I will often get good grades.
Good grades make me feel happy.

(5)

If I do my best, I will usually get good grades.
Everyone is proud of me when I do my best.

(7)

When my grade is not so good, I might feel sad.
But, I can always try again.
I will ask my teacher to help me.

(6)

I will work on meeting
my goal - 10 ✔'s!

Make a ✔ each time you read your story.

by ________________________

A lockdown drill helps me practice what to do if the school is not safe.

③

(2) At my school, we have drills to practice
how to stay safe in an emergency.
One drill we practice is called a lockdown.

I should remember that most of the time, this is just practice.
We practice having a lockdown in case there is a problem.

When there is a lockdown drill, my teacher will tell me what to do.
I will listen to my teacher.

(5)

It is very important that I listen to my teacher.
Whatever my teacher says, I will do it quickly.

(7)

My teacher will lock the door of my classroom.
She will turn off the lights.
She will lock the windows and pull down the blinds.

 6

I will need to stay inside my classroom.
This means I cannot get a drink or use the restroom for a while.

8

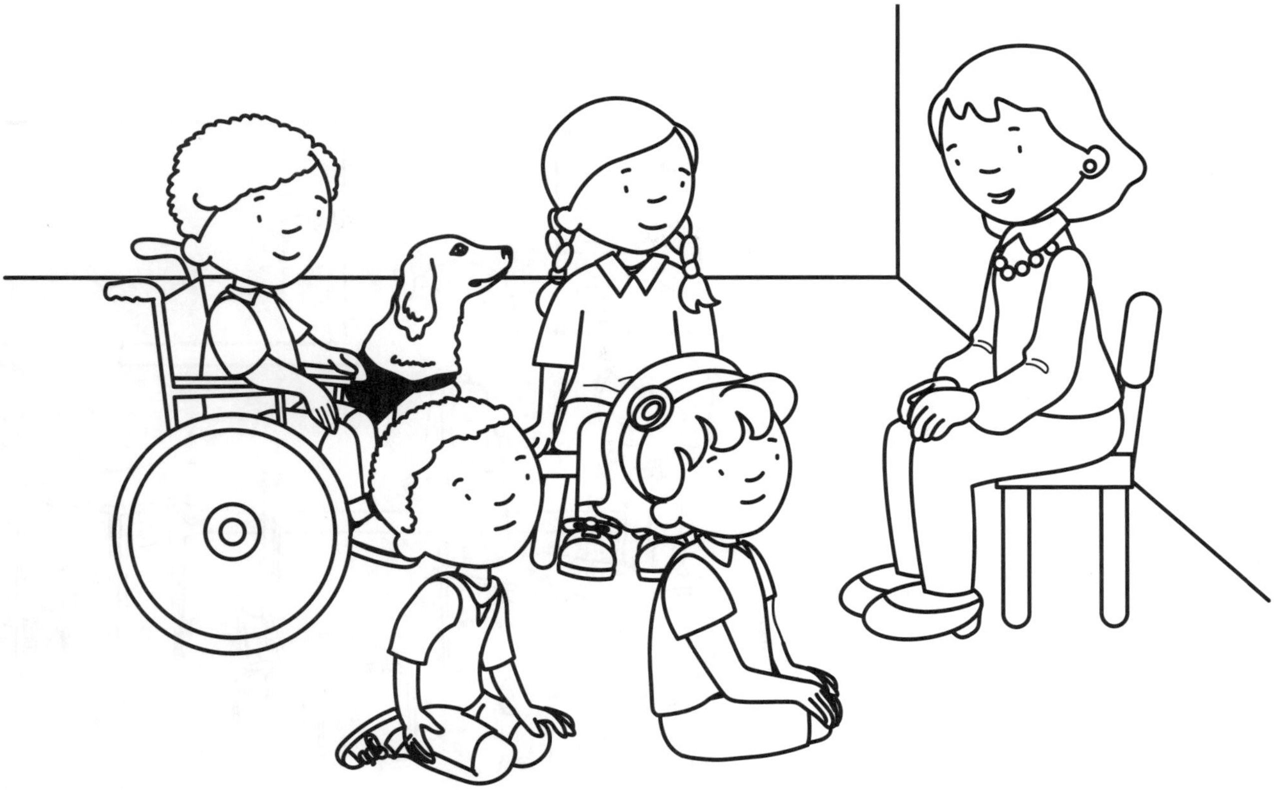

I will sit on the floor with my friends.
I will sit very quietly and wait.

$\textbf{9}$

I do not need to be afraid during a lockdown drill.
My class and I are practicing how to be safe at school.
It is important to be safe at school.

$\textbf{11}$

(10) Lockdown drills do not last for very long.
I will wait until my teacher tells me the drill is over.

I will work on meeting
my goal - 10 ✔'s!

Make a ✔ each time you read your story.

by ________________________________

It is important to know what to do if there is a fire.
That is why we practice.

3

(2) We have drills to practice how to stay safe in school.
One drill is called a fire drill.

We do not always know when there is going to be a fire drill.
It will probably be a surprise.

(4)

We will hear the alarm and see the flashing lights.
The alarm will ring, and it will be very loud.
The lights will flash, and they will be very bright.

(5)

When the alarm rings, I will get out of my seat.
I do not have to put my things away or finish my work.

(7)

6

I do not like loud noises.
And, this is a very loud noise.
But, it is important to hear the alarm bell.

8

It is OK to stop what I am doing.
I will get in line with my class.

When I am in line, I will be quiet.
I will walk in a straight line behind my teacher.

(9)

I do not need to be afraid during a fire drill.
My class and I are practicing how to be safe at school.
It is important to be safe at school.

(11)

(10) My class always goes outside when there is a fire drill.
I will stay with my teacher until she says it is safe to go inside.

I will work on meeting
my goal - 10 ✔'s!

Make a ✔ each time you read your story.

WHOO-RAY!!

____
Name

KNOWS OUR SCHOOL ROUTINES.

_______________________   _______________________
Signed   Date

High Flyer
Award
Name
has completed each school
routine story with flying colors!
Signed
Date
© Carson Dellosa • KE-804118
62
© Carson Dellosa

by_____________________________________

I will work on meeting
my goal - 10 ✔'s!

Make a ✔ each time you read your story.
